Fo... ...ina
De...
(...

Panna

12 | 28 | 2022

SEARCHING FOR HOME

Haiku
by
Panna Naik

NAP NEW ACADEMIA PUBLISHING   SCARITH
Washington DC

Printed in the United States of America

Library of Congress Control Number: 2022915559

ISBN 978-1-955835-37-4 paperback (alk. paper)

 An imprint of New Academia
Publishing

New Academia Publishing
4401-A Connecticut Avenue NW
Washington DC
info@newacademia.com
www.newacademia.com

For
Grace Cavalieri
With much affection and great admiration

Where Basho and Dickinson Meet—
An Introduction

Pamela Sutton

Panna Naik's brief, redolent book of Haiku resounds like a "Titanic Opera." So much is spoken in so few words, which is the mission of the boldest Haiku. Imagine, for a moment, if Basho hadn't skirted the direct duties of his family's farm to study Haiku and its iterations with Yoshitada? Then, after his first poetry teacher, Yoshitada, died, imagine if Basho had not begun his walking journeys and written down his observations of life. Our world would be a lesser place.

Right now, our world, our planet, is on fire. The permafrost is melting. STEM: Science; Technology; Engineering; and Math—this is all we are allowed to push upon our school children. I, too, love science: neutrinos swooshing above, below, and through me each breath I take; but I also love Basho's Frog: *"The old pond—A frog jumped in,—Kerplunk!"* (tr. Allen Ginsberg); which is the embodiment of neutrinos.

I grew up next to a pond teeming with frogs, and the pond was fenced around with ancient willows streaming with lemon-colored leaves. The frogs were my friends; the pond was their home. It was 1966. I was 6.

My 9-year-old friend, Mike, brought his bb-gun down to the pond and began teaching me how to shoot frogs. At first it was interesting, then immediately nauseating, as I observed my handiwork: all of my frog-friends belly-up and bleeding, washed by banners of willow leaves weeping.

Keen observation is everything: seeing until it hurts. If all Poets; indeed, if all Humanity, could experience Panna Naik's daily observations: the way she steps lightly; feel her severe sensitivity, which damages nothing, we would already have a healthier planet and a more peaceful world.

The same year I was born, 1960, a young woman journeyed from India to America.

She brought with her "mystical visions and cosmic vibrations": *"Does the maple tree— remember—its birthplace?"*. These visions followed her wherever she walked: *"Butterfly perched—on windshield—Love letter."*

Like so often happens with great Poets and intellects, Panna worked collateral to Academia, but not directly in it. Certainly, she was an essential Professor in South Asian Studies. She is the University of Pennsylvania's Librarian Emerita. She holds three Master's degrees, but not a PhD. And Bravo for her, I say: neither did Emily Dickinson nor Basho. But here, in this laser-focused book of Haiku, Dickinson and Basho surely meet and stare at each other in wonder.

They look down at our green-blue planet. They watch forest fires rage, while frogs gasp for oxygen and die. They watch our wars, particularly this new one in Europe. They say, STEM is fine and well, but if you want to survive as a species, you must teach the children poetry again.

Start with this book.

Acknowledgments

Publication of any book is a collaborative process. This book is no exception. I am grateful to numerous people who have been variously helpful to me in writing, revising and promoting this book:

At New Academia Publishing, Anna Lawton, took personal interest in the book and ably shepherded it all the way to its publication as she had done for my earlier book, *The Astrologer's Sparrow* (2018).

Two highly accomplished literary friends Mira Desai and Roshni Kearns Rustomji as well as Jenna Lordo closely read and edited an earlier version of the manuscript and helped me rewrite and organize various poems.

Grace Cavalieri, the noted poet and Poet Laureate of the State of Maryland has consistently supported me with her encouragement and good words.

She recommended the publication of this book as well as the earlier one, *The Astrologer's Sparrow* (2018).

The distinguished poet Pamela Sutton wrote a generous foreword.

Apurva Ashar of Navajivan Press designed and made the book look beautiful and very eye pleasing.

And above all, Natwar Gandhi, my life partner, who reads everything I write and nearly always improves it.

Needless to say, despite all of the help I received from these good people, I am sure there are still unavoidable shortcomings in the book for which I hold only myself responsible.

A Dew Sufficed Itself

A DEW sufficed itself
And satisfied a leaf,
And felt, 'how vast a destiny!
How trivial is life!'
The sun went out to work,
The day went out to play,
By physiognomy.
Whether by day abducted,
Or emptied by the sun
Into the sea, in passing,
Eternally unknown.

—Emily Dickinson

April's air stirs in
Willow-leaves...a butterfly
Floats and balances.

—Basho

Why the moment
I wear shoes
New grass quivers.

Vast, salty
Ocean, fish
Weeping.

Love hangs
Against the wall
Frozen photograph.

Etched inside
Window frame
Piece of sky.

Suffocating
Crowd
My loneliness.

I get up
Dusting grass-grit
From my clothes.

Dawn: the house
Delighted and chaotic
With sunbeams.

Like rough gravel
Underfoot
Separation stings.

Sunshine dappled wall
Of many paintings
The breeze works its brush.

Late evening
Wind fumbles for keys
In slumbering grass.

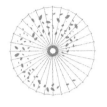

The butterfly delights
Deep velvet carpet
Of flowers.

The thirsty afternoon
Pants on a dog's
Lolling tongue.

Grains of sand
Count eternity
Between two waves.

Wind's plea
To the candle flame
Be steady, steady!

Sunlight steps through
Window to table
Sip of tea.

A sunbeam
Struck my foot
At the threshold.

Chattering streams
Crowded woods
An empty bench.

Flirting with me
Time
Got off scot-free!

This wrinkle free
Sheet of solitude
Never worn nor shared.

The sunflower alters
Its heart
With the sun's direction.

We lit up
The dead of night
With beacons of words.

Dusk: a riot
Of sunbeams gambols
On tender grass.

Sunset sadness
Lengthened with
The rising moon.

Grass carpet
Betrayed my feet,
Not the stone!

The train departs
I cannot wave
My wet handkerchief.

Sunlight slides
Each evening
Downhill slopes.

The butterfly folds
Its wings, sleeps
In sunflower's lap.

Warm sunlight
Splashes
In a puddle.

The lavish sky
Took all its water
Wealth for granted.

Bruising its cloudy head
The wind struggles
To open that closed window.

Calendar pages
Ruffled by the fan
Silences the wall.

At first blink
Silk sheen of dreams
Slip away.

Your love
Creased
Like a handkerchief.

Is it night or you?
Slipping away
From my embrace?

Despite
The desert's blowing dust
Fresh flowers.

As soon as you get up
Timid bangles
Tremble.

Lipstick
Stains
My teacup's brim.

In this formal park
Trees sway
To wind's song.

Threshold too tall
For infant sunlight
To crawl over.

Breath moans
Inside
Air-conditioned towers.

Grass blades bend
Bearing
The butterfly's weight.

The radiant earth
Wears a veil
Of tender grass shoots.

Blinded!
Too many tears
Blur my eyes.

A drowsy afternoon
Snuggles
On a jade pond.

The moon reigns
Over a court
Of stars.

Sunlight
Soaks up wet
Footprints.

Turmeric-anointed
Daffodils grow and heal
Beneath a canopy of grass.

A nimble doe
Untamable
Memory.

The butterfly's
Mute scream
At dead flowers.

Wings as oars
Swans swim
In the sky lake.

Wrinkles
On faces or love
Cannot be removed.

The city drenched
In moonlight's
Torrential deluge.

Dream affair
Escapes
Shut eyelashes.

Black-robed night
A jury of stars
Accused the day.

A dewdrop
Etches patterns
On a rose petal.

Winter sunlight shivers
And hunts the house
For a quilt.

Dawn
Leaves whisper
The wind's prayer.

Sun and wind
Slash
The tree trunk.

Sunshine jumps
On the grass
Yellow rabbit.

Sunshine sleeps
On branch bed
Flower pillow.

A sunray stepped in
With a brush
Painting the walls.

Moonlight rolls over
Caressing
The bedsheet.

Where will a fish
Tired from swimming
Find rest in the sea?

Thoughts thread
Slowly, daintily
Like a ladybug.

A cuckoo's trills
Rang out
In the garden.

Blizzard
Snowflakes dance to
The beating winds.

Shimmering fish
Pulses of light
On still waters.

My mind takes flight
With a kite
Dull meeting.

Stars gathered
Searching for the moon
Ink-black night.

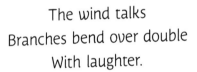

The wind talks
Branches bend over double
With laughter.

Only one bird took flight
But the entire tree
Trembled.

Words thread
Night
Stitching the darkness.

Handwriting smudges
Damp letter
With memories.

A downpour
Of torrential fog
Flooded the hills.

Plucking a flower
A dewdrop painted
My nail.

In the midst of chaos
Our eyes speak
Serenely.

The toothless mouth
Ruminates
Times long gone.

So thirsty for the moon
The ocean
Frothed at its mouth.

Footprints of small clouds
Ran all over
The windshield.

Stealthy wind
Seeps
Through a window crack.

That one photo
Taken off the wall
So much space.

Life-long search
For the brush
To paint my dreams.

Under a grass canopy
Flowers envy
The butterflies.

Where will birds perch?
When branches break
One after another.

The panting train
Halts at the station
To catch its breath.

It's public knowledge
My love-affair
With poetry.

I don't fear death,
Just the warm embrace
Of poetry.

Wind races
To gather night lilies
Water trembles.

Rain song
Thunder drums
Lightning dances.

Butterflies ask the grass:
Can you bear
Our weight?

Bright birds
Colorful bird chatter
I see every hue.

Each tree, each branch
Sways
To a new beat.

Wet streets
Moonlight's feet
Won't get dusty tonight.

White rabbits wander
Grazing sunlight
On a grass carpet.

Empty garden
Only the chatter
Of the lawnmower.

Flower
Another name
For a tree's smile.

The brazen wind
Embraces
A fresh bud.

Time closes in on me
Demanding
An account.

Fish swim
To my pulse.
Is my body an ocean?

Playful ocean wave
Erases
Footprints.

Not rain but
A downpour of moonlight
Drums the tiled rooftop.

Clouds hover
On wind's wings
Scintillant sky.

Drenched
In the torrent
Of memory's deluge.

Letter peeps
From the mailbox
Eyes well up.

Stroking its feathers
The sun
Awakens the bird.

You are arriving
The rumor
Spread by flowers.

I could leap over hills
To meet him
But threshold too high.

Facing the roaring ocean
Sand grains harden
Eyes wide open.

Not the night lily,
But a lyric shoots forth
From moonlit lake.

Waste of inhalation
No aroma
Artificial flowers.

Page after ecstatic page
Sewn with living thread
Predestined ties.

Unraveling, remeasuring
Folding and folding
The cloth bolt of time.

Gibbous moon
Ignited waves
Crest.

Why the door?
If there is no greeting
Nor farewell.

Does the maple tree
Remember
Its birthplace?

The moment
Fingers touch the still waters
Stars disperse.

The tree trembles, ecstatic
With excitement
Or fear?

A butterfly lands
On windshield
A love letter.

Kissing the palm
Already kissed
Reliving moments.

Why do fish panic
Under the skin
Of the ocean?

Vase of flowers shatters
Fragrance spills
Into the carpet.

Lake water creases
Wind's wand
Writes poetry.

Drooping branches
Pull the sky down
Pluck stars.

Wring the tear-soaked handkerchief
Over the well
Then measure the level!

Fish wander
Midocean
Searching for home.

Panna Naik

A distinguished Gujarati poet, Ms. Panna Naik has been active on Gujarati literary front for about four decades and has established herself as a major writer. She has written several volumes of path breaking poetry and short stories and has given a distinct voice to Indian women as evidenced by her world-wide following. Her poetry has been amply recognized and awarded by Gujarati literary establishment both in India and here. Recently she published The Astrologer's Sparrow a volume of poetry in English.

In addition, she has also done pioneering work in the teaching of Gujarati language and taught second generation students for years in her capacity as Adjunct Professor at the University of Pennsylvania.

CPSIA information can be obtained
at www.ICGtesting.com
Printed in the USA
JSHW051024161222
34837JS00005B/97